Y0-ARU-809

Edwin A. Abbey

"Hung round the bowers, and fondly look'd their last"

The Deserted Village

A POEM WRITTEN BY

Oliver Goldsmith

AND ILLUSTRATED BY

Edwin A. Abbey R.A.

New York & London
Harper & Brothers
Publishers 1902

Published October, 1902.

INTRODUCTION

WAS Goldsmith's "deserted village" Lissoy, in the county of Westmeath, in the kingdom of Ireland; or was it Kennaquhair, in Dream County, Poet Land? The Rev. R. H. Newell, B.D., and Fellow of St. John's College, Cambridge, maintains that it was Lissoy. In 1811 he published a quarto volume of Goldsmith's *Poetical Works,* the chief object of which was to support this proposition. He referred to the fact that Chaucer had depicted Woodstock in the "Cuckoo and the Nightingale" (which, unfortunately for the Rev. R. H. Newell, is not now regarded as Chaucer's), and he instanced the resemblance traced by Sir William Jones (how far off Sir William Jones seems as a critic!) between a passage in "L'Allegro" and a landscape near Oxford. He, too, had found resemblances. He had himself been to Lissoy. He had discovered there a "never-failing brook" and a "busy mill," just as they are in Goldsmith's time-honored line; and he was satisfied that the "decent church that topt the neighboring hill" —seeing that churches on hills are so exceptional—could (clearly) be none other than the church of Kilkenny West as seen from Lissoy Parsonage. Moreover, he found a hawthorn-tree, or rather the stump thereof, which in its umbrageous days had evidently been admirably adapted for "talking age" and "whispering lovers"; and in the little mount of Knockaruadh he recognized unhesitatingly the eminence indicated in the passage:

"Sweet was the sound when oft, at evening's close,
Up yonder hill the village murmur rose;
There, as I past, with careless steps and slow,
The mingling notes came soften'd from below:
The swain responsive as the milkmaid sung,
The sober herd that low'd to meet their young;
The noisy geese that gabbled o'er the pool,
The playful children just let loose from school;"

and so forth, filling "each pause the nightingale had made." In like fashion, the school-house, the village inn, the smithy are all identified for us by this amiable enthusiast. He has even sketched them, in the obsolete drawing-book manner of Paul Sandby and the first water-colorists, and had them reproduced in aquatint by Alken. One has to "make believe" a good deal in order to detect in these bare and amateurish designs the sources of Goldsmith's images. Like his own "fair female," they are decidedly "unadorn'd and plain," and, borrowing his own words once more, "imagination" has "to stoop" (and stoop considerably) if it is to distinguish Auburn in the lineaments of Lissoy. A mill, a tree, a hill scarcely fix its locality. If, as Goldsmith tells us, the "seats of his youth" really lingered in his memory, they must have been wholly transfigured in the enchanted haze of a regretful retrospect. And he was well placed at that period where distance adds its charm to contemplation, for nearly twenty years—years unusually chequered—had passed over his head since, starting for Edinburgh, he had left forever the little hamlet of his boyhood on the road from Ballymahon to Athlone.

He himself, if one knows him at all, whatever may have been his obligations to his native environment, would probably have resented too nice an identification of Auburn with Lissoy. He had become "Dr." Goldsmith. He was a member of the Literary Club. He had been appointed Professor of History to the Royal Academy; and he was the author of "The Traveller," a philosophical and didactic poem. As a "philosophical and didactic poem" he chiefly valued "The Deserted Village." It was not upon his exquisite little *genre* pictures — not upon his portraits of the clergyman and the village school-master — not upon his vignette of that

> "sad historian of the pensive plain,"

the aged water-cress-gatherer, that he prided himself most. It was upon the passages which treat of depopulation, and the alleged cause of depopulation — luxury — that he relied. Nowadays we care least for these. We doubt his conclusions, as Johnson did; we are even not quite sure about his facts. But not so Goldsmith. "Sir," one can imagine him saying—as, indeed, he does say to Reynolds in his admirable "Dedication"—"I sincerely believe what I have written. I have taken all possible pains, in my country excursions, for these four or five years past, to be certain of what I allege. All my views and inquiries have led me to believe those miseries real which I here attempt to display." And then, if Johnson were not present to rout his self-possession by a thundering "Why, no, sir," or other ejaculation of offence, he would probably go on to trace it all to his favorite source, and perhaps would quote, in his queer, halting, but not unfeeling utterance, his own verses:

> "Thus fares the land, by LUXURY betray'd;
> In nature's simplest charms at first array'd,
> But verging to decline, its splendors rise,
> Its vistas strike, its palaces surprise;

INTRODUCTION

> While, scourg'd by famine from the smiling land,
> The mournful peasant leads his humble band;
> And while he sinks, without one arm to save,
> The country blooms—a garden, and a grave."

Yes, he had seen these things. But, as Macaulay says, he had not seen them together. His "smiling village" was English; his evictions were Irish. His mistake was that (like the gentleman who wrote on Chinese metaphysics) he had combined his information, and so "produced something which never was and never will be seen in any part of the world."

At Lissoy, however, it was not unnatural that so complimentary a tradition should find its adherents. Indeed, one of the poet's admirers, a Mr. Hogan, who christened his house "Auburn," went so far as to rebuild or repair the old ale-house at Lissoy, and to equip it with the sign of the "Three Jolly Pigeons." Furthermore, he restored or supplied the properties of the ale-house in the poem. Whether it actually had its

> "chest contriv'd a double debt to pay—
> A bed by night, a chest of drawers by day,"

we know not; but it certainly had

> "The white-wash'd wall, the nicely sanded floor,
> The varnish'd clock that click'd behind the door,"

as well as

> "The pictures plac'd for ornament and use,
> The twelve good rules, the royal game of goose."

Nor, says Goldsmith's laborious first biographer. Prior, were wanting the

> "broken teacups, wisely kept for show,"

which glistened over the chimney, but for some occult reason were firmly embedded in the mortar—a circumstance which did not prevent their being stolen, together with the sign, by relic-hunters. But perhaps the most interesting thing about Mr. Hogan's renovated hostelry is the fact that, to the unsympathetic eye of criticism, it is just those very objects by which he sought to establish the identity of the inn at Auburn and the inn at Lissoy which are most assailable by a heartless incredulity. Oddly enough, some twelve years before, when he was living miserably in Green Arbour Court, Goldsmith had submitted to his brother Henry a sample of a heroi-comic poem describing a Grub Street writer in bed in "a paltry ale-house." In this "the sanded floor," the "twelve good rules," and the broken teacups all played their parts as accessories, and even the double-dealing chest had its prototype in the poet's night-cap, which was "a cap by night—a stocking all the day."

A year or two later he expanded these lines in the *Citizen of the World,* and the scene becomes the Red Lion in Drury Lane. From this second version he adapted, or extended again, the description of the inn parlor in "The Deserted Village." It follows, therefore, either that he borrowed for London the details of a house in Ireland, or that he used for Ireland the details of a house in London. If, on the other hand, it be contended that those details were common to both places, then the identification in these particulars of Auburn with Lissoy falls hopelessly to the ground.

Something of the same treatment may be applied to the characters of the poem. It is frequently stated that the school-master is a recollection of his own first master at Lissoy, Thomas or "Paddy" Byrne. That some of Byrne's traits are probably repeated in the picture may be admitted, but a closer examination tends to reduce even these to a minimum. Byrne, as described by Goldsmith's sister, was a character so individual that, if Goldsmith intended to depict him, he must be held to have failed conspicuously. Byrne had been a quartermaster under Peterborough in Spain; he had travelled over a great part of Europe, and seen strange things by sea and land, returning to his native village with an unabated taste for a wandering life, and an infinite faculty for relating his experiences. To the little, thick-set, and, by all accounts, thick-witted boy whom he instructed or endeavored to instruct in "the Three R's," the story of his personal perils was a never-failing source of delight. Nor was Byrne entirely limited to those narratives in which (metaphorically speaking) he "shoulder'd his crutch, and show'd how fields were won"; he had an inexhaustible supply of legends of fairies and banshees, and he was an adept in the swarming chap-book literature of his day. There is nothing of all this in the pedagogue of "The Deserted Village." Goldsmith might have depicted that worthy just as well if he had never heard of Paddy Byrne, never listened to his tales of Fair Rosamond and Tom Hickathrift, or his memories of "the great Rapparee chiefs, Baldearg O'Donnell and galloping Hogan." Paddy Byrne may have been "severe, and stern to view," though one would scarcely expect it from his other characteristics; he may have been able to presage "times and tides," and even have used "words of learned length and thundering sound." But it is evident that, if these were among his peculiarities, Goldsmith must have intentionally neglected his essential features in order to seize upon certain characteristics which he possessed in common with a great many people. Indeed, if it were not, as Fluellen says, "to mock at an honorable tradition," now too long established to be eradicable, it might be contended that Goldsmith never thought of Paddy Byrne at all, but simply built up "out of scraps and heel-taps" of observation and experience and memory what the world has since recognized as an almost typical picture of a village school-master.

It is probable, however, that there is more in the story which connects the village clergyman, also rather a type than a character, with certain members of the poet's own family, who, at the time he wrote, had all become part of his youth and of an irrevocable past. But the very discordance of the identification seems to show conclusively that no one figure sat by itself for the picture. Mrs. Hodson, Goldsmith's sister, for example, maintained that it was the likeness of her father. "The Rev. Charles Goldsmith," she wrote, "is allowed by all that knew him to have been faithfully represented by his son in the character of the Village Preacher in his poem." Others found the true original in Goldsmith's brother Henry, the brother to whom, turning nobly from a noble patron, he had dedicated "The Traveller." "It will also throw a light upon many parts of it," he says, "when the reader understands that it is addressed to a man who, despising Fame and Fortune, has retired early to Happiness and Obscurity, with an income of forty pounds a year." If the amount of the stipend is to decide the question, then this is exactly the amount upon which the parson of the poem was "passing rich." Unfortunately it was also the stipend of many other country curates—of Charles Churchill, for instance—in whom we should certainly not seek for Goldsmith's model. A third claimant has been put forward in the person of the Rev. Thomas Contarine, that kind and long-suffering uncle to whom the poet owed so deep a debt of gratitude. It was Uncle Contarine who had assisted him at school and college; Contarine who had established him as a tutor; Contarine who had equipped him fruitlessly for the law; and Contarine who had finally supplied the funds to enable him to study medicine at Edinburgh. But the truth is that he drew from none of these individually, though he may have borrowed traits from each. That they were all kindly, modest, simple, unambitious, generous, is probably true; but it is impossible to dissociate from them a certain weakness and want of fibre which are frequently found in combination with these amiable qualities. To what he saw in them Goldsmith added a dignity, a moral grandeur, which again exalts the character to the type. Of Charles Goldsmith it might be said truly that "his house was known to all the vagrant train," for his son has told us so; of his brother Henry that he "nor e'er had chang'd, nor wish'd to change, his place"—a statement which the dedication to "The Traveller" supports; of his uncle Contarine that he was "more skilled to raise the wretched than to rise." But not to one, or to any of these separately, belong those noble concluding lines which for so many years have been regarded as the *ne varietur* representation of a typical village pastor—a picture for a parallel to which one must travel back some four hundred years to Chaucer's "poor parson of a town":

> "Beside the bed where parting life was laid,
> And sorrow, guilt, and pain by turns dismay'd,
> The reverend champion stood. At his control,
> Despair and anguish fled the struggling soul;
> Comfort came down the trembling wretch to raise,
> And his last faltering accents whisper'd praise.
>
> "At church, with meek and unaffected grace,
> His looks adorn'd the venerable place;
> Truth from his lips prevail'd with double sway,
> And fools who came to scoff remain'd to pray.
> The service past, around the pious man,
> With steady zeal, each honest rustic ran;
> Even children follow'd with endearing wile,
> And pluck'd his gown, to share the good man's smile.
> His ready smile a parent's warmth exprest,
> Their welfare pleas'd him, and their cares distrest;
> To them his heart, his love, his griefs were given,
> But all his serious thoughts had rest in heaven.
> As some tall cliff that lifts its awful form,
> Swells from the vale, and midway leaves the storm,
> Though round its breast the rolling clouds are spread,
> Eternal sunshine settles on its head."

That branch of criticism which busies itself with parallel passages has been unusually active with respect to the deservedly admired simile with which the foregoing lines conclude, chiefly, it would appear, with the view of proving that it could not possibly have been Goldsmith's own. It is not improbable that it was; and, indeed, it might plausibly be contended, in a controversy in which so much is taken for granted, that he himself expanded it, by the ordinary operations of imagination, from his own line in "The Traveller" where he describes himself as "plac'd on high above the storm's career." But it is certainly noteworthy that so many passages have been discovered which might have suggested it. We pass by Claudian, Lucan, Statius —all of whom have been named—because, in all likelihood, if Goldsmith found it anywhere, he found it nearer home. But the first Lord Lytton called attention to a passage from Chaulieu which certainly has much affinity to Goldsmith's lines. An even closer parallel was pointed out in 1886 by a correspondent in the *Academy,* from Chapelain's "Ode to Richelieu":

> "*Dans un paisible mouvement*
> *Tu t'élèves au firmament,*
> *Et laisses contre toi murmurer cette terre;*
> *Ainsi le haut Olympe, à son pied sablonneux,*
> *Laisse fumer la foudre et gronder la tonnerre,*
> *Et garde son sommet tranquille et lumineux.*"

There is also, as Mitford shows, a passage in Young's

"Night Thoughts" which, in an incondite way, foreshadows the idea:

> "As some tall Tow'r or lofty Mountain's Brow
> Detains the Sun, Illustrious from its Height,
> While rising Vapours, and descending Shades,
> With Damps and Darkness drown the Spatious Vale:
> Undampt by Doubt, Undarken'd by Despair,
> *Philander*, thus, augustly rears his Head."

That Goldsmith may have met with both of these is not unlikely. He knew Young and Young's works, and in "Edwin and Angelina" quoted a couplet from the same source as that above cited. He was also thoroughly familiar, probably as a result of his wanderings in France, with the French minor poets of the seventeenth and eighteenth centuries, to whom his obligations, acknowledged and unacknowledged, are not inconsiderable. Either in Chapelain or Young or Chaulieu he had probably made mental note of the passage, and retained it so long that it had become an undistinguishable part of his own imaginative equipment. This is not an unusual occurrence, nor is it the only one in Goldsmith. The line, "A breath can make them, as a breath has made," is an almost textual reproduction of an old French motto upon an hour-glass, which Victor Hugo is also said to have unconsciously repeated; and the famous simile in "The Traveller" of the separation that "drags, at each remove, a lengthening chain," is but a memory of Cibber, who "conveyed" it from Dryden. That Goldsmith got it from Cibber is probable from the fact that another well-known saying of his is traced to the same source. When he said of Johnson that, "when his pistol missed fire, he knocked you down with the butt end," he was only saying what—as Boswell is careful to inform us—Cibber had said before him in one of his comedies. There is another example of his curious mental method in the "Good-Natur'd Man." Years before, in the *Enquiry into the Present State of Polite Learning,* he had quoted Sir William Temple's exquisite likening of life to "a froward child, that must be humored and coaxed a little till it falls asleep, and then all care is over." When Goldsmith first used this he gave it as a quotation from an unnamed author; by the time his first comedy was written, he had adopted the foundling of his brain, and puts it without acknowledgment into the lips of Croaker.

As in the case of "The Traveller," several of the couplets in "The Deserted Village" have their first form in the poet's prose works. If there is no line textually repeated, like "A land of tyrants and a den of slaves" in the earlier poem, there are more than one of the couplets which recall passages both in the *Citizen of the World* and the *Vicar of Wakefield.* But the closest parallel is a paragraph of "A

City Night Piece," an essay printed in the *Bee*, and then repeated in one of Lien Chi's epistles: "These poor shivering females have once seen happier days and been flattered into beauty. . . . Perhaps now lying at the doors of their betrayers, they sue to wretches whose hearts are insensible, or debauchees who may curse, but will not relieve them." In "The Deserted Village" this is obviously and happily expanded in the touching—

"Are these thy serious thoughts? Ah! turn thine eyes
Where the poor houseless shivering female lies.
She once, perhaps, in village plenty blest,
Has wept at tales of innocence distrest;
Her modest looks the cottage might adorn,
Sweet as the primrose peeps beneath the thorn;
Now lost to all, her friends, her virtue fled,
Near her betrayer's door she lays her head,
And, pinch'd with cold, and shrinking from the shower,
With heavy heart deplores that luckless hour
When idly first, ambitious of the town,
She left her wheel and robes of country brown."

It has been already said that, in spite of rumors to the contrary, Goldsmith never returned to Lissoy. But to the last he was always intending to go back. "I am again just setting out for Bath," he writes in one of his letters, "and I honestly say I had much rather it had been for Ireland with my nephew, but that pleasure I hope to have before I die." This is practical proof that his wish was never fulfilled, for the words were written in the last years of his life; and they are also practical proof that, whether Lissoy was or was not the "deserted village," he desired to revisit the "seats of his youth." To this feeling he has consecrated what are perhaps the most genuinely tender and yearning of his verses:

> "In all my wanderings round this world of care,
> In all my griefs—and GOD has given my share—
> I still had hopes, my latest hours to crown,
> Amidst these humble bowers to lay me down;
> To husband out life's taper at the close,
> And keep the flame from wasting by repose:
> I still had hopes, for pride attends us still,
> Amidst the swains to show my book-learn'd skill,
> Around my fire an evening group to draw,
> And tell of all I felt, and all I saw;
> And, as a hare whom hounds and horns pursue,
> Pants to the place from whence at first he flew,
> I still had hopes, my long vexations past,
> Here to return—and die at home at last."

These, again, have their prose expression in the *Citizen of the World*: "However we toil, or wheresoever we wander, our fatigued wishes still recur to home for tranquillity; we long to die in that spot which gave us birth, and in that pleasing expectation opiate every calamity."

In some memorable lines with which he concluded his work he bade adieu to Poetry. She was unfit, he said, in that degenerate time, to "touch the heart"—one of her functions upon which, as an unregarded critic, he had insisted, even in those blank days of his bondage to Griffiths the bookseller. She was "his shame in crowds; his solitary pride"; and he further apostrophizes her as—

> "Thou source of all my bliss and all my woe,
> Thou found'st me poor at first, and keep'st me so."

Whether he sincerely intended to abandon the Muse may be a moot point. There is often in such official severances no more than a wistful craving to test the actual position—to savor by anticipation the sweets of a quasi-posthumous repute—to excite in advance the grateful homage of regret. But whatever were Goldsmith's real feelings upon the subject, his words, in two respects, proved strictly accurate. "The Deserted Village" was really his last serious poetical effort. The "Threnodia Augustalis" is admittedly a mere occasional piece, while "Retaliation" was the outcome of an accident. Nor is there reason for supposing that he himself would have published any of the verses which appeared after his death, although two of them, "The Haunch of Venison" and the "Letter in Prose and Verse to Mrs. Bunbury," are among his most popular productions. What he regarded as his poetical works proper were "The Hermit," "The Traveller," and "The Deserted Village," those pieces, in fact, upon which he had labored most assiduously—"the rest is all but leather or prunello"—and to this vein of poetry he did, in fact, bid good-bye, whether he meant it or not.

The other respect in which his words were no literary fiction is the fact that, great as was his reputation, his verse "kept him poor." His process of composition was languid and fastidious; his final touches lingering and far between. If a well-known anecdote is to be taken literally, he considered from four to ten lines a good morning's work—a rate of progression which approaches the "incredible slowness" of Malherbe or Waller. Yet for "The Traveller" he got but twenty guineas, and for "The Deserted Village" a hundred. Such remuneration must naturally keep him poor, and it is not wonderful that he should have fallen back upon the easy, perspicuous prose, which he wrote so readily and so inimitably. That, in the circumstances, he should have written poetry at all is remarkable; that in the "dead season" between Gray and Cowper he should have left behind him a piece of work so beautiful, so tender in touch, and so enduring as "The Deserted Village" is more remarkable still. There is no surer proof that the Muses are truly to some, as the Latin poet has it, *dulces ante omnia*—sweet beyond aught else.

AUSTIN DOBSON.

EALING, *August*, 1902.

TO SIR JOSHUA REYNOLDS

DEAR SIR,—

I can have no expectations, in an address of this kind, either to add to your reputation or to establish my own. You can gain nothing from my admiration, as I am ignorant of that art in which you are said to excel; and I may lose much by the severity of your judgment, as few have a juster taste in poetry than you. Setting interest, therefore, aside, to which I never paid much attention, I must be indulged at present in following my affections. The only dedication I ever made was to my brother, because I loved him better than most other men. He is since dead. Permit me to inscribe this poem to you.

How far you may be pleased with the versification and mere mechanical parts of this attempt, I do not pretend to inquire; but I know you will object (and, indeed, several of our best and wisest friends concur in the opinion) that the depopulation it deplores is nowhere to be seen, and the disorders it laments are only to be found in the poet's own imagination. To this I can scarcely make any other answer than that I sincerely believe what I have written; that I have taken all possible pains, in my country excursions, for these four or five years past, to be certain of what I allege; and that all my views and inquiries have led me to believe those miseries real which I here attempt to display. But this is not the place to enter into an inquiry whether the country be depopulating or not; the discussion would take up much room, and I should prove myself, at best, an indifferent politician to tire the reader with a long preface when I want his unfatigued attention to a long poem.

In regretting the depopulation of the country, I inveigh against the increase of our luxuries; and here also I expect the shout of modern politicians against me. For twenty or thirty years past, it has been the fashion to consider luxury as one of the greatest national advantages; and all the wisdom of antiquity in that particular as erroneous. Still, however, I must remain a professed ancient on that head, and continue to think those luxuries prejudicial to states by which so many vices are introduced and so many kingdoms have been undone. Indeed, so much has been poured out of late on the other side of the question that, merely for the sake of novelty and variety, one would sometimes wish to be in the right.

I am, dear sir,

Your sincere friend and ardent admirer,

OLIVER GOLDSMITH.

"The Deserted Village, a Poem by Dr. Goldsmith. London: Printed for W. Griffin, at Garrick's Head, in Catharine Street, Strand, 1770, 4to," was first published in May, 1770, and ran through six editions in the same year in which it was first published. The price was *2s.*

ILLUSTRATIONS

ILLUSTRATIONS

ILLUSTRATIONS

THE DESERTED VILLAGE

A Poem

"How often have I loiter'd o'er thy green"

THE DESERTED VILLAGE

Sweet Auburn! loveliest village of the plain,

Where health and plenty cheer'd the laboring swain

Where smiling spring its earliest visit paid,

And parting summer's lingering blooms delay'd;

Dear lovely bowers of innocence and ease,

Seats of my youth, when every sport could please,

How often have I loiter'd o'er thy green,

Where humble happiness endear'd each scene!

How often have I paus'd on every charm,—

The shelter'd cot, the cultivated farm,

The never-failing brook, the busy mill,

The decent church that topt the neighboring hill,

The hawthorn bush, with seats beneath the shade,

For talking age and whispering lovers made![1]

How often have I blest the coming day,[2]

When toil remitting lent its turn to play,

"The decent church that topt the neighboring hill"

And all the village train, from labor free,

Led up their sports beneath the spreading tree;

While many a pastime circled in the shade,

The young contending as the old survey'd;

And many a gambol frolick'd o'er the ground,

And sleights of art and feats of strength went round!

And still as each repeated pleasure tir'd,

Succeeding sports the mirthful band inspir'd;

The dancing pair that simply sought renown,

By holding out to tire each other down;

The swain, mistrustless of his smutted face,

While secret laughter titter'd round the place;

The bashful virgin's sidelong looks of love,

The matron's glance that would those looks reprove.

These were thy charms, sweet village! sports like these,

With sweet succession, taught even toil to please;

"The hawthorn bush, with seats beneath the shade"

These round thy bowers their cheerful influence shed,

These were thy charms—but all these charms are fled.

Sweet smiling village, loveliest of the lawn,

Thy sports are fled, and all thy charms withdrawn;

Amidst thy bowers the tyrant's hand is seen,[3]

And desolation saddens all thy green:

One only master grasps the whole domain,

And half a tillage stints thy smiling plain;

No more thy glassy brook reflects the day,

But, chok'd with sedges, works its weedy way;

Along thy glades, a solitary guest,

The hollow-sounding bittern guards its nest;[4]

Amidst thy desert walks the lapwing flies,

And tires their echoes with unvaried cries.

Sunk are thy bowers in shapeless ruin all,

And the long grass o'ertops the mouldering wall;

"When every rood of ground maintain'd its man"

And, trembling, shrinking from the spoiler's hand,

Far, far away thy children leave the land.

Ill fares the land, to hastening ills a prey,

Where wealth accumulates, and men decay:

Princes and lords may flourish, or may fade—

A breath can make them, as a breath has made;

But a bold peasantry, their country's pride,

When once destroy'd, can never be supplied.

A time there was, ere England's griefs began,

When every rood of ground maintain'd its man;

For him light labor spread her wholesome store,

Just gave what life requir'd, but gave no more:

His best companions, innocence and health,

And his best riches, ignorance of wealth.

But times are alter'd; trade's unfeeling train

Usurp the land, and dispossess the swain:

"And every pang that folly pays to pride"

Along the lawn where scatter'd hamlets rose,

Unwieldy wealth and cumbrous pomp repose;

And every want to opulence allied,[5]

And every pang that folly pays to pride.

Those gentle hours that plenty bade to bloom,

Those calm desires that ask'd but little room,

Those healthful sports that grac'd the peaceful scene,

Liv'd in each look, and brighten'd all the green.

These, far departing, seek a kinder shore,

And rural mirth and manners are no more.

Sweet Auburn! parent of the blissful hour,

Thy glades forlorn confess the tyrant's power.

Here, as I take my solitary rounds,

Amidst thy tangling walks and ruin'd grounds,

And, many a year elaps'd, return to view

Where once the cottage stood, the hawthorn grew,[6]

"Around my fire an evening group to draw"

Remembrance wakes, with all her busy train,

Swells at my breast, and turns the past to pain.

In all my wanderings round this world of care,

In all my griefs—and God has given my share—

I still had hopes, my latest hours to crown,

Amidst these humble bowers to lay me down;

To husband out life's taper at the close,

And keep the flame from wasting by repose:[7]

I still had hopes, for pride attends us still,

Amidst the swains to show my book-learn'd skill,

Around my fire an evening group to draw,

And tell of all I felt, and all I saw;

And, as a hare whom hounds and horns pursue,

Pants to the place from whence at first he flew,

I still had hopes, my long vexations past,

Here to return—and die at home at last.[8]

"Nor surly porter stands in guilty state"

"The swain responsive as the milkmaid sung"

O blest retirement, friend to life's decline,

Retreats from care, that never must be mine,

How happy he who crowns, in shades like these,[9]

A youth of labor with an age of ease;

Who quits a world where strong temptations try,

And, since 'tis hard to combat, learns to fly!

For him no wretches, born to work and weep,

Explore the mine, or tempt the dangerous deep;

Nor surly porter stands in guilty state,

To spurn imploring famine from the gate:

But on he moves to meet his latter end,

Angels around befriending Virtue's friend;

Bends to the grave with unperceiv'd decay,[10]

While Resignation gently slopes the way;

And, all his prospects brightening to the last,

His heaven commences ere the world be past.[11]

"The sober herd that low'd to meet their young"

Sweet was the sound when oft, at evening's close,

Up yonder hill the village murmur rose;

There, as I past with careless steps and slow,

The mingling notes came soften'd from below:

The swain responsive as the milkmaid sung,

The sober herd that low'd to meet their young;

The noisy geese that gabbled o'er the pool,

The playful children just let loose from school;

The watch-dog's voice, that bay'd the whispering wind,

And the loud laugh that spoke the vacant mind—

These all in sweet confusion sought the shade,

And fill'd each pause the nightingale had made.

But now the sounds of population fail,

No cheerful murmurs fluctuate in the gale;

No busy steps the grass-grown footway tread,

For all the bloomy flush of life is fled—

"The sad historian of the pensive plain"

All but yon widow'd, solitary thing,

That feebly bends beside the plashy spring;

She, wretched matron—forc'd in age, for bread,

To strip the brook with mantling cresses spread,

To pick her wintry fagot from the thorn,

To seek her nightly shed, and weep till morn—

She only left of all the harmless train,

The sad historian of the pensive plain.[12]

Near yonder copse, where once the garden smil'd,

And still where many a garden flower grows wild;

There, where a few torn shrubs the place disclose,

The village preacher's modest mansion rose.[13]

A man he was to all the country dear,

And passing rich with forty pounds a year.

Remote from towns he ran his godly race,

Nor e'er had chang'd, nor wish'd to change, his place;

"His house was known to all the vagrant train"

Unpractis'd he to fawn,[14] or seek for power,

By doctrines fashion'd to the varying hour;

Far other aims his heart had learn'd to prize,

More skill'd to raise[15] the wretched than to rise.

His house was known to all the vagrant train,

He chid their wanderings, but reliev'd their pain;

The long-remember'd beggar was his guest,

Whose beard descending swept his aged breast;

The ruin'd spendthrift, now no longer proud,

Claim'd kindred there, and had his claims allow'd;

The broken soldier, kindly bade to stay,

Sat by his fire, and talk'd the night away;

Wept o'er his wounds, or, tales of sorrow done,

Shoulder'd his crutch, and show'd how fields were won.

Pleas'd with his guests, the good man learn'd to glow,

And quite forgot their vices in their woe;

"Beside the bed where parting life was laid"

Careless their merits or their faults to scan,

His pity gave ere charity began.

Thus to relieve the wretched was his pride,

And even his failings lean'd to Virtue's side;

But in his duty prompt at every call,

He watch'd and wept, he pray'd and felt for all

And, as a bird each fond endearment tries

To tempt its new-fledg'd offspring to the skies,

He tried each art, reprov'd each dull delay,

Allur'd to brighter worlds, and led the way.

Beside the bed where parting life was laid,

And sorrow, guilt, and pain by turns dismay'd,

The reverend champion stood. At his control,

Despair and anguish fled the struggling soul;

Comfort came down the trembling wretch to raise,

And his last faltering accents whisper'd praise.

"His looks adorn'd the venerable place"

At church, with meek and unaffected grace,

His looks adorn'd the venerable place;

Truth from his lips prevail'd with double sway,

And fools who came to scoff remain'd to pray.[16]

The service past, around the pious man,

With steady zeal, each honest rustic ran;

Even children follow'd with endearing wile,

And pluck'd his gown, to share the good man's smile.

His ready smile a parent's warmth exprest,

Their welfare pleas'd him, and their cares distrest;

To them his heart, his love, his griefs were given,

But all his serious thoughts had rest in heaven.

As some tall cliff that lifts its awful form,

Swells from the vale, and midway leaves the storm,

Though round its breast the rolling clouds are spread,

Eternal sunshine settles on its head.

"A man severe he was, and stern to view"

"I knew him well, and every truant knew"

Beside yon straggling fence that skirts the way,

With blossom'd furze unprofitably gay,

There, in his noisy mansion, skill'd to rule,

The village master taught his little school.

A man severe he was, and stern to view;

I knew him well, and every truant knew:

Well had the boding tremblers learn'd to trace

The day's disasters in his morning face;

Full well they laugh'd with counterfeited glee

At all his jokes, for many a joke had he;

Full well the busy whisper, circling round,

Convey'd the dismal tidings when he frown'd.

Yet he was kind, or, if severe in aught,

The love he bore to learning was in fault.

The village all declar'd how much he knew;

'Twas certain he could write, and cipher too;

"At all his jokes, for many a joke had he"

Lands he could measure, terms and tides presage,

And even the story ran—that he could gauge:

In arguing, too, the parson own'd his skill,

For even though vanquish'd, he could argue still;

While words of learned length and thundering sound

Amaz'd the gazing rustics rang'd around;

And still they gaz'd, and still the wonder grew

That one small head could carry all he knew.[17]

But past is all his fame. The very spot
Where many a time he triumph'd is forgot.
Near yonder thorn, that lifts its head on high,
Where once the sign-post caught the passing eye,
Low lies that house where nut-brown draughts inspir'd,
Where graybeard mirth and smiling toil retir'd,
Where village statesmen talk'd with looks profound,
And news much older than their ale went round.

"While words of learned length and thundering sound"

Imagination fondly stoops to trace

The parlor splendors of that festive place:

The whitewash'd wall, the nicely sanded floor,

The varnish'd clock that click'd behind the door;[18]

The chest contriv'd a double debt to pay—

A bed by night, a chest of drawers by day;

The pictures plac'd for ornament and use,

The twelve good rules, the royal game of goose;

The hearth, except when winter chill'd the day,

With aspen boughs, and flowers, and fennel gay,

While broken teacups, wisely kept for show,

Rang'd o'er the chimney, glistened in a row.[19]

Vain, transitory splendors! could not all

Reprieve the tottering mansion from its fall?

Obscure it sinks, nor shall it more impart

An hour's importance to the poor man's heart.

"The parlor splendors of that festive place"

Thither no more the peasant shall repair

To sweet oblivion of his daily care;

No more the farmer's news, the barber's tale,

No more the woodman's ballad shall prevail;

No more the smith his dusky brow shall clear,

Relax his ponderous strength, and lean to hear;

The host himself no longer shall be found

Careful to see the mantling bliss go round;

Nor the coy maid, half willing to be prest,

Shall kiss the cup to pass it to the rest.

Yes! let the rich deride, the proud disdain,

These simple blessings of the lowly train;

To me more dear, congenial to my heart,

One native charm than all the gloss of art:

Spontaneous joys, where nature has its play,

The soul adopts, and owns their first-born sway;

"Relax his ponderous strength, and lean to hear"

Lightly they frolic o'er the vacant mind,

Unenvied, unmolested, unconfin'd.

But the long pomp, the midnight masquerade,

With all the freaks of wanton wealth array'd,

In these, ere triflers half their wish obtain,

The toiling pleasure sickens into pain:

And, even while fashion's brightest arts decoy,

The heart distrusting asks, if this be joy.

Ye friends to truth, ye statesmen who survey
The rich man's joys increase, the poor's decay,
'Tis yours to judge how wide the limits stand
Between a splendid and a happy land.[20]
Proud swells the tide with loads of freighted ore,
And shouting Folly hails them from her shore;
Hoards even beyond the miser's wish abound,
And rich men flock from all the world around.

"The host himself no longer shall be found"

Yet count our gains. This wealth is but a name,

That leaves our useful products still the same.

Not so the loss. The man of wealth and pride

Takes up a space that many poor supplied—

Space for his lake, his park's extended bounds,

Space for his horses, equipage, and hounds:

The robe that wraps his limbs in silken sloth,

Has robb'd the neighboring fields of half their growth;

His seat, where solitary sports are seen,

Indignant spurns the cottage from the green;

Around the world each needful product flies

For all the luxuries the world supplies.

While thus the land, adorn'd for pleasure all,

In barren splendor feebly waits the fall.

As some fair female, unadorn'd and plain,

Secure to please while youth confirms her reign,

"Nor the coy maid, half willing to be prest"

"But the long pomp, the midnight masquerade,
With all the freaks of wanton wealth arrayed"

Slights every borrow'd charm that dress supplies,

Nor shares with art the triumph of her eyes;

But when those charms are past, for charms are frail,

When time advances, and when lovers fail,

She then shines forth, solicitous to bless,

In all the glaring impotence of dress:

Thus fares the land, by luxury betray'd;

In nature's simplest charms at first array'd,

But verging to decline, its splendors rise.

Its vistas strike, its palaces surprise;

While, scourg'd by famine from the smiling land,

The mournful peasant leads his humble band;

And while he sinks, without one arm to save,

The country blooms—a garden, and a grave.

Where then, ah! where shall poverty reside,

To scape the pressure of contiguous pride?

". . . . The man of wealth and pride
Takes up a space that many poor supplied—"

If to some common's fenceless limits stray'd,
He drives his flock to pick the scanty blade,
Those fenceless fields the sons of wealth divide,
And even the bare-worn common is denied.

If to the city sped—what waits him there?
To see profusion that he must not share;
To see ten thousand baneful arts combin'd
To pamper luxury, and thin mankind;

To see those joys the sons of pleasure know,[21]

Extorted from his fellow-creatures' woe.

Here, while the courtier glitters in brocade,

There the pale artist plies the sickly trade;

Here, while the proud their long-drawn pomps display,

There the black gibbet glooms beside the way.

The dome where Pleasure holds her midnight reign,

Here, richly deck'd, admits the gorgeous train;

"As some fair female, unadorn'd and plain,
Secure to please while youth confirms her reign"

Tumultuous grandeur crowds the blazing square,

The rattling chariots clash, the torches glare.

Sure scenes like these no troubles e'er annoy!

Sure these denote one universal joy!

Are these thy serious thoughts? Ah! turn thine eyes

Where the poor houseless shivering female lies.

She once, perhaps, in village plenty blest,

Has wept at tales of innocence distrest;

Her modest looks the cottage might adorn,

Sweet as the primrose peeps beneath the thorn;

Now lost to all, her friends, her virtue fled,

Near her betrayer's door she lays her head,[22]

And, pinch'd with cold, and shrinking from the shower,

With heavy heart deplores that luckless hour

When idly first, ambitious of the town,

She left her wheel and robes of country brown.

"She then shines forth, solicitous to bless,
In all the glaring impotence of dress"

Do thine, sweet Auburn, thine, the loveliest train
Do thy fair tribes participate her pain?
Even now, perhaps, by cold and hunger led,
At proud men's doors they ask a little bread!

Ah, no. To distant climes, a dreary scene,
Where half the convex world intrudes between,
Through torrid tracts with fainting steps they go,
Where wild Altama[23] murmurs to their woe.

Far different there from all that charm'd before,

The various terrors of that horrid shore;

Those blazing suns that dart a downward ray,

And fiercely shed intolerable day;

Those matted woods where birds forget to sing,

But silent bats in drowsy clusters cling;

Those poisonous fields with rank luxuriance crown'd,

Where the dark scorpion gathers death around;

"There the pale artist plies the sickly trade"

Where at each step the stranger fears to wake

The rattling terrors of the vengeful snake;

Where crouching tigers[24] wait their hapless prey,

And savage men more murderous still than they;

While oft in whirls the mad tornado flies,

Mingling the ravag'd landscape with the skies.

Far different these from every former scene,

The cooling brook, the grassy-vested green,

The breezy covert of the warbling grove,

That only sheltered thefts of harmless love.

Good Heaven! what sorrows gloom'd that parting day,

That call'd them from their native walks away;

When the poor exiles, every pleasure past,

Hung round the bowers, and fondly look'd their last,

And took a long farewell, and wish'd in vain

For seats like these beyond the Western main;

"Sweet as the primrose peeps beneath the thorn"

And, shuddering still to face the distant deep,

Return'd and wept, and still return'd to weep!

The good old sire, the first prepar'd to go

To new-found worlds, and wept for others' woe;

But for himself, in conscious virtue brave,

He only wish'd for worlds beyond the grave.

His lovely daughter, lovelier in her tears,

The fond companion of his helpless years,

Silent went next, neglectful of her charms,

And left a lover's for a father's arms.[25]

With louder plaints the mother spoke her woes,

And blest the cot where every pleasure rose;

And kiss'd her thoughtless babes with many a tear,

And clasp'd them close, in sorrow doubly dear;

Whilst her fond husband strove to lend relief

In all the silent manliness of grief.[26]

"Near her betrayer's door she lays her head"

"Down where yon anchoring vessel spreads the sail"

O Luxury! thou curst by Heaven's decree,

How ill exchang'd are things like these for thee!

How do thy potions, with insidious joy,

Diffuse their pleasures only to destroy!

Kingdoms by thee, to sickly greatness grown,

Boast of a florid vigor not their own:

At every draught more large and large they grow,

A bloated mass of rank unwieldy woe;

Till, sapp'd their strength, and every part unsound,

Down, down they sink, and spread a ruin round.

Even now the devastation is begun,

And half the business of destruction done;

Even now, methinks, as pondering here I stand,

I see the rural Virtues leave the land.

Down where yon anchoring vessel spreads the sail,

That idly waiting flaps with every gale,

" Downward they move—a melancholy band—"

Downward they move, a melancholy band,

Pass from the shore, and darken all the strand.

Contented toil, and hospitable care,

And kind connubial tenderness, are there;

And piety with wishes plac'd above,

And steady loyalty, and faithful love.

And thou, sweet Poetry, thou loveliest maid,

Still first to fly where sensual joys invade;

Unfit, in these degenerate times of shame,

To catch the heart, or strike for honest fame;

Dear charming nymph, neglected and decried,

My shame in crowds, my solitary pride;

Thou source of all my bliss and all my woe,

Thou found'st me poor at first, and keep'st me so;

Thou guide by which the nobler arts excel,

Thou nurse of every virtue, fare thee well!

"Thou found'st me poor at first, and keep'st me so"

Farewell, and oh, where'er thy voice be tried,

On Torno's cliffs or Pambamarca's side,[27]

Whether where equinoctial fervors glow,

Or winter wraps the polar world in snow,

Still let thy voice, prevailing over time,

Redress the rigors of the inclement clime;

Aid slighted truth with thy persuasive strain;

Teach erring man to spurn the rage of gain;

Teach him that states of native strength possest,

Though very poor, may still be very blest;

That trade's proud empire hastes to swift decay,

As ocean sweeps the labor'd mole away;

While self-dependent power can time defy,

As rocks resist the billows and the sky.[28]

NOTES

[1] "Lissoy, near Ballymahon, where the poet's brother, a clergyman, had his living, claims the honor of being the spot from which the localities of 'The Deserted Village' were derived. The church which tops the neighboring hill, the mill, and the brook, are still pointed out; and a hawthorn has suffered the penalty of poetical celebrity, being cut to pieces by those admirers of the bard who desired to have classical tooth-pick cases and tobacco-stoppers. Much of this supposed locality may be fanciful, but it is a pleasing tribute to the poet in the land of his fathers."—SIR WALTER SCOTT, *Miscellaneous Prose Works*, vol. iii. p. 250, ed. 1834.

[2] Supposed to allude to the number of saints' days in Ireland, kept by the Roman Catholic peasantry.

[3] The "tyrant" said to be intended in this and other passages was Lieutenant-General Robert Napier (or Naper, as his name was more frequently written), an English gentleman who, on his return from Spain, purchased an estate near Ballymahon, and ejected many of his tenants for non-payment of their rents.

[4] "Those who have walked in an evening by the sedgy sides of unfrequented rivers must remember a variety of notes from different water-fowl—the loud scream of the wild-goose, the croaking of the mallard, the whining of the lapwing, and the tremulous neighing of the jacksnipe; but of all these sounds, there is none so dismally hollow as the booming of the bittern. It is impossible for words to give those who have not heard this evening call an adequate idea of its solemnity. It is like an interrupted bellowing of a bull, but hollower

and louder, and is heard at a mile's distance, as if issuing from some formidable being that resided at the bottom of the waters. I remember, in the place where I was a boy, with what terror this bird's note affected the whole village: they considered it as a presage of some sad event, and generally found or made one to succeed it."—*History of Animated Nature,* vol. vi. p. 24.

[5] "And every want to *luxury* allied."

First Edition, altered in Third.

[6] Here followed, in the first, second, and third editions:

"Here, as with doubtful, pensive steps I range,
Trace every scene, and wonder at the change,
Remembrance," etc.

[7] "My anxious day to husband near the close,
And keep life's flame from wasting by repose."

First, Second, and Third Editions.

[8] "Towards the decline of his life he [Waller] bought a small house with a little land at Coleshill, and said 'he should be glad to die like the stag—where he was roused.' This, however, did not happen."—JOHNSON, *Life of Waller.*

[9] "How blest is he who crowns, in shades like these."

First Edition, altered in Third.

[10] "Sinks to the grave with unperceiv'd decay."

First Edition, altered in Third.

[11] Watson's large engraving (1772), after Sir Joshua Reynolds's picture of "Resignation," is thus inscribed: "This attempt to express a character in 'The Deserted Village' is dedicated to Dr. Goldsmith by his sincere friend and admirer, JOSHUA REYNOLDS."

[12] The "sad historian of the pensive plain" (whose figure is to be seen on the copper-plate vignette of the editions published in Goldsmith's lifetime) was, it is said, Catherine Geraghty, of Lissoy. The brook and ditches near the spot where her cabin stood still furnish cresses, and several of her descendants were residing in the village in 1837.

[13] The "village preacher" was, it is said, the poet's father—so,

at least, his sister, Mrs. Hodson, believed; but the poet's brother, and his uncle Contarine, have both been named as the originals of this delightful character.

[14] " Unskilful he to fawn."—*First Edition, altered in Fifth.*

[15] " More bent to raise."—*First Edition, altered in Fifth.*

[16] " Our vows are heard betimes, and Heaven takes care
To grant before we can conclude the pray'r;
Preventing angels met it half the way,
And sent us back to praise who came to pray."

DRYDEN, *Britannia Rediviva.*

[17] Goldsmith is here supposed to have drawn the portrait of his own early instructor, Mr. Thomas Byrne, a retired quartermaster of an Irish regiment that had served in Marlborough's wars.

[18] " Goldsmith's chaste pathos makes him an insinuating moralist, and throws a charm of Claude-like softness over his descriptions of homely objects that would seem only fit to be the subjects of Dutch painting. But his quiet enthusiasm leads the affections to humble things without a vulgar association; and he inspires us with a fondness to trace the simplest recollections of Auburn, till we count the furniture of its ale-house, and listen to the 'varnish'd clock that click'd behind the door."—CAMPBELL, *British Poets,* vol. vi. p. 263.

[19] An ale-house, on the supposed site of this, in the Deserted Village, and with the sign of " The Three Jolly Pigeons " (in honor, doubtless, of Tony Lumpkin), was rebuilt or repaired by Mr. Hogan, the poet's relative.—PRIOR'S *Life,* ii. 265.

[20] " Happy, very happy, might they have been, had they known when to bound their riches and their glory. Had they known that extending empire is often diminishing power; that countries are ever strongest which are internally powerful; that colonies, by draining away the brave and enterprising, leave the country in the hands of the timid and the avaricious; . . . that too much commerce may injure a nation as well as too little; and that there is a wide difference between a conquering and a flourishing empire."—*The Citizen of the World,* Letter xxv.

NOTES

[21] " To see each joy," etc.—*First Edition, altered in Third.*

[22] " These poor shivering females have once seen happier days, and been flattered into beauty. They have been prostituted to the gay luxurious villain, and are now turned out to meet the severity of winter. Perhaps, *now lying at the doors of their betrayers,* they sue to wretches whose hearts are insensible, or debauchees who may curse, but will not relieve, them."—*The Citizen of the World,* Letter cxvii.

[23] A river in Georgia; properly Altamaha, and pronounced Oltamahaw.

[24] The jaguar, or American tiger, is unknown on the banks of the Altamaha.

" I believe I have taken a poetical license to transplant the *jackal* from Asia. In Greece I never saw nor heard these animals; but among the ruins of Ephesus I have heard them by hundreds. They haunt ruins and follow armies."—LORD BYRON, *Siege of Corinth,* note.

[25] " And left a lover's for *her* father's arms."
First, Second, and Third Editions.

[26] " In all the decent manliness of grief."
First, Second, and Third Editions.

[27] The river Torneå falls into the Gulf of Bothnia. Pambamarca is a mountain near Quito.

[28] " Dr. Johnson favored me, at the same time, by marking the lines which he furnished to Goldsmith's ' Deserted Village,' which are only the last four."—BOSWELL by Croker, p. 174.

THE END